CONTENTS

The Booklet

The Posters

HOUSE OF TUDOR

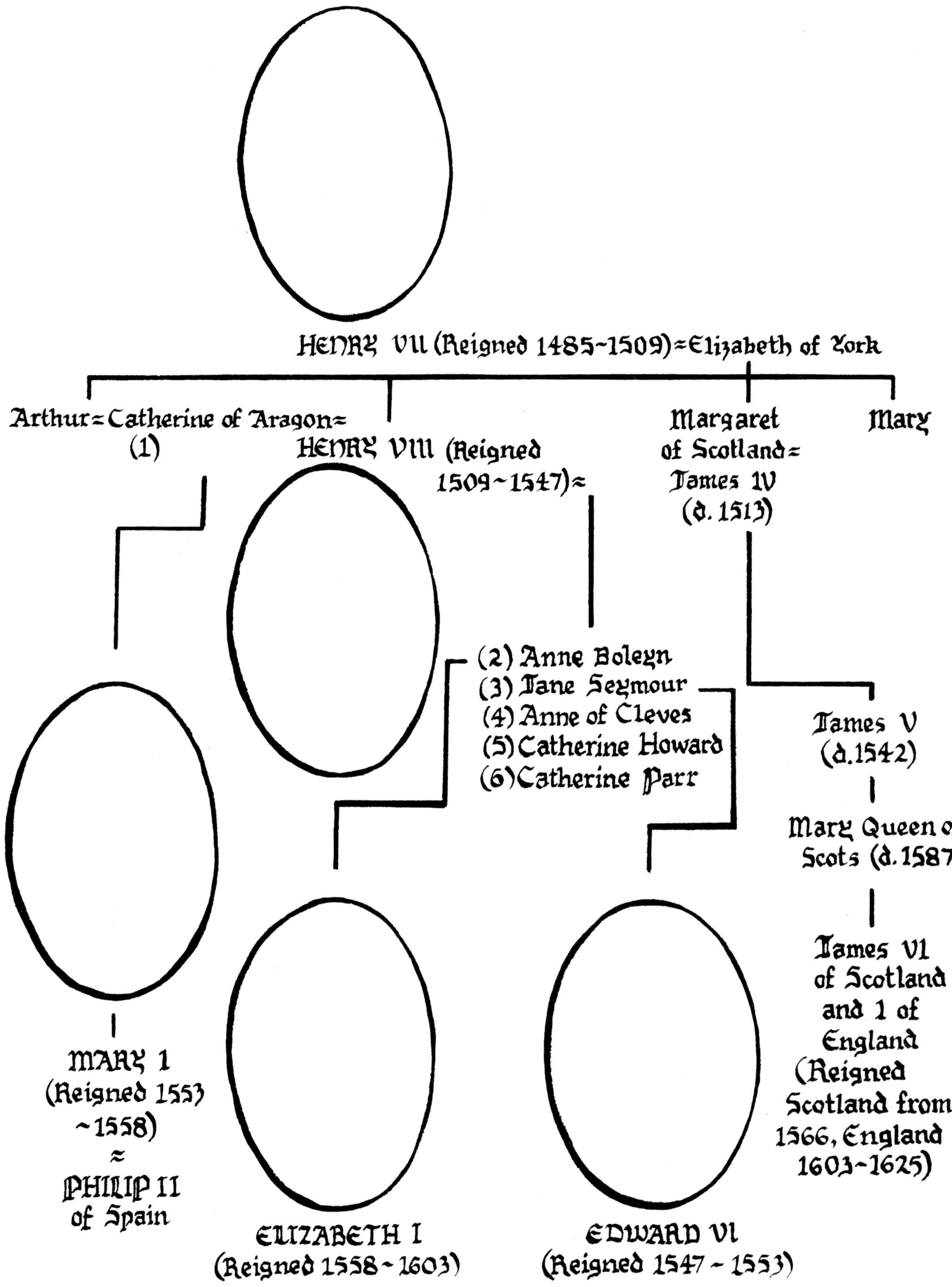

Introduction

The pictures in this pack are among the most important images produced in Tudor England. Between them they convey a wealth of historical information about the Tudor period. They range from major statements of royal power (Henry VIII and Elizabeth I) to a mourning widow's desire to commemorate her dead husband (Sir Henry Unton). While several of these pictures are by unknown painters, the pack includes a drawing by the finest artist to work in England during the entire sixteenth century, the German Hans Holbein the Younger. Most of the images included here are extremely large, but the portrait of Henry VII, painted for a potential bride contemplating matrimony, is of a small enough size to be carried across Europe for her inspection.

The medium used for all the paintings is oil paint, but the supports vary from wooden panels, mainly used in the earlier period, to canvas during the latter years of Elizabeth's reign; Holbein's drawing is in ink and watercolour on paper.

Based on the teaching practices of the National Portrait Gallery's Education Department, this resource pack shows how portraits can be used as historical sources.

Ideal for teachers working with Key Stage 2 pupils, the information provided here can be adapted for both older and younger children. In addition, though it has particular relevance to Key Stage 2 History – Study Unit 2: 'Life in the Tudor Times', this pack also includes cross-curricular activities including art, English, geography and maths.

Designed for ease of use, the booklet consists of logical discussions for each of the images reproduced as posters. These notes include an introduction to each image, written at teacher-level and designed to provide background information which should be read before taking the session (*italic text*). Alongside this is a structured class discussion, which provides relevant questions which teachers should ask their class or group. Suggested pupil answers are given in brackets – it may be necessary to add extra questions to help develop discussion. Additional information, which must be fed into the session, is shown in boxes – it is clearly indicated where this information should be introduced. Suggested activities relating to each picture or topic are also included, with black-and-white photocopy masters provided to help facilitate practical exercises.

The portraits in this pack can be tackled in any order. However, as an introduction to Tudor portraits in general, pupils should discuss the following questions:

Why did the Tudors have portraits made of themselves?

(To establish themselves as important persons, to show off their wealth and status, as decoration, to commemorate particular events, for example, coronations. The fact that photography was not an option available to them should also be mentioned.)

What sort of people had portraits made?

(Essentially rich people, they were quite expensive. This limits their usefulness as historical evidence.)

What materials were used?

(Wooden or canvas supports and oil paint. This question can be further extended to explore the minerals used to make pigments, if desired.)

ACTIVITY

Make miniature paintings of the Tudor Dynasty and add to the Tudor Family tree (**photocopy master 1**). You will need to refer to other books to complete this activity. The National Portrait Gallery's range of Tudor portraits on slide, poster and postcard would also help in this exercise.

Henry VII

Attributed to Michiel Sittow, 1505

INTRODUCTION

This portrait of Henry VII played a part in a marriage negotiation. As the inscription records, it was painted on 20 October 1505 by order of Herman Rinck, agent of the Holy Roman Emperor Maximilian I. Henry hoped to marry Maximilian's daughter Margaret of Austria, as his second wife, after the death of Elizabeth of York. This portrait of Henry was sent to her in exchange for two portraits of herself. Margaret kept the painting until her death; it is plausibly attributed to Michiel Sittow who was the Duchess's court painter.

Henry is shown as a European monarch, wearing the Order of the Golden Fleece awarded to him by Maximilian. The rose he holds symbolises the Tudor dynasty and is also a symbol of a prospective lover.

STRUCTURED DISCUSSION

Focus on the purpose of this portrait

How were portraits used to help arrange royal marriages in Tudor times?

(Discussion could cover Holbein's painting of Anne of Cleves used in the marriage negotiations with Henry VIII and their subsequent divorce.)

When Margaret received this painting of Henry VII, do you think it made her want to marry him?

(No, probably not.)

This picture was used in marriage negotiations between Henry VII and Margaret of Austria. It was commissioned by Margaret's father so they could find out what Henry VII looked like. Michiel Sittow was sent to England to paint the picture and bring it back with him.

Focus on how Henry is presented

What is he holding?

(A red rose, symbol of the Tudor dynasty and love.)

In what ways does he show his wealth?

(The rich fabric of his gown, the fur collar, the gold chain.)

Do you think that this is a flattering portrait of Henry, or a realistic one?

(Realistic, the artist was working for Margaret.)

Focus on the style of the painting

How has the painter made Henry appear as though he is looking through a window?

(Sky blue background, shape of the picture, hands resting on the sill.)

What is this portrait painted on?

(Wooden panel.)

What type of paint has been used?

(Oil paint.)

Focus on flattery

Compare this portrait with the image of Henry VII in the *Whitehall Cartoon* (see **poster 2** and the detail of Henry VII

In *The Whitehall Cartoon* Holbein presents Henry VII as a typical Renaissance monarch. Henry VII was dead by the time Holbein settled in England in 1532, but he was able to use the tomb sculpture of Henry VII in Westminster Abbey to find out what the dead king looked like – the tomb itself is a flattering image.

The Holbein portrait is a good example of flattery in Tudor portraiture; the vast majority of Tudor portraits flatter the sitter. Another way to detect flattery is to compare the painted portrait with a written, contemporary description of the sitter, although writing can be biased too. Here is a description of Henry VII from Polydore Vergil's *Anglica Historia*, which Henry commissioned in 1505 (the same year as the painting):

'His figure was slim but well built and strong; in height he was above average. Extremely attractive in appearance, his face was cheerful, especially when he was speaking. He had small, blue eyes, a few poor black-stained teeth. His hair was thin and white: his complexion sallow.'

in **photocopy master** 2) to examine the idea of flattery in portraiture.

Compare the noses. What differences do you see?

(The Sittow portrait has a thin, hooked nose; in the Holbein it is wider and more dignified.)

Compare the eyes. What differences do you see?

(Smaller in the Sittow than in the Holbein.)

Compare the hair. What differences do you see?

(Wispier and thinner in the Sittow.)

Compare the shapes of the faces. What differences do you see?

(Very pronounced cheekbones in the Sittow; fuller in the Holbein.)

Compare the lips. What differences do you see?

(Very thin in the Sittow.)

Compare the general differences. What do you notice?

(Younger and more handsome in the Holbein than in the Sittow.)

ACTIVITIES

1. Make another painted portrait of Henry VII intended to flatter him.
2. Write a letter from Henry VII to Margaret of Austria in which he tells her about himself and tries to persuade her to marry him.

Henry VIII *and* **Henry VII** *(The Whitehall Cartoon)*

By Hans Holbein the Younger, 1536–1537

INTRODUCTION

Holbein's sophisticated and vivid portraits were greatly admired, and dominated English Court taste from 1532. It has been calculated that one-fifth of all the nobility of Henry VIII's time sat to Holbein. The English courtiers were the first to realise that 'we be constrayned if we wyll have any thinge well paynted kerved or embrawded to abandon our own countrymen and resorte unto strangers [foreigners]*.' As painter to Henry VIII, Holbein's most important public function was to present the monarch as a mighty Renaissance prince. From 1536 to 1537, he did just this by producing a wall painting for the Privy Chamber of Whitehall Palace in London. The palace burned down in 1698, destroying the painting; fortunately it had been copied earlier in the century by Remigius van Leemput* (**photocopy master 3**) *(though not particularly well: it is possible that the apparent change to the tilt of Henry VII's head is really just poor copying). Holbein's preparatory cartoon for the left-hand side of the mural has, however, survived. (The term for a detailed preparatory drawing like this is a cartoon!)*

Henry's body, though visually striking, has some anatomical peculiarities in Holbein's ➳

STRUCTURED DISCUSSION

Focus on the familiarity of the images

Who are these two people?

(Henry VII and Henry VIII.)

Whom did you recognise more easily?

(Generally Henry VIII.)

When you picture Henry VIII in your mind, does he look like this, but in colour?

(Usually yes.)

Focus on Henry VIII

Did Henry VIII really look like this?

(Introduce the idea of flattery – see discussion of *Henry VII* by Michiel Sittow.)

How do his clothes help to flatter his figure?

(Wide shoulders to balance his large stomach.)

> A lot of people do think of Henry VIII as looking like this portrait. This is the image that the artist Hans Holbein created for Henry, and it shows Henry as he wanted to be remembered. It is a bit like creating advertisements today.

What messages about himself is Henry VIII giving us in the picture?

(Power, authority, strength, wealth, masculinity/virility.)

How does the picture convey these messages?

(Wealth: ornate clothes, jewels, elaborate background; strength: size of Henry VIII, his pose and dagger; power/authority: his facial expression and pose, positioning of Henry VIII in front of his father and in the foreground of the picture; masculinity/virility: size of Henry VIII, codpiece.)

Focus on how this picture was made

The image is drawn in ink with a light coat of watercolour; what is it drawn on?

(Paper, although you cannot tell this from the poster, most people guess correctly from general knowledge.)

> Try standing in the same position as Henry VIII, to show how the pose accentuates size and strength.

image: the elongation of his legs is deliberate flattery (you can see this clearly if you compare the drawing with his suit of armour in the Tower of London), and his right arm is very oddly angled, though the impossibility of this position is masked by the padding on his shoulder.

Holbein's powerful image of kingship was copied many times, and has conditioned the way we perceive Henry VIII. It has been highly effective propaganda over the last 400 years.

To make the mural, Holbein had to transfer the image of the cartoon on to a wall in Whitehall Palace. In order to transfer the essential outlines of a drawing, Holbein would use one of two methods. Tracing was the method he most commonly favoured. To ensure a clear transfer, a second sheet of paper, coated on one side with charcoal or dark chalk, would be placed beneath the drawing, with the coated side facing down onto the panel. The drawing would then be firmly traced, and the image would be clearly transferred to the panel as if by carbon paper. Before applying paint, Holbein would then reinforce the transferred image on the panel with brush or charcoal following the gradations of tone recorded by his chalk and ink drawings and written notes. ➳

This is a preparatory drawing for a wall painting in Henry's palace in Whitehall (see Introduction). The finished wall painting was in colour but was destroyed in a fire in 1698 and only this part has survived.

Could they make a piece of paper this size in Tudor times?

(No, several pieces are glued together.)

How could you transfer a drawing like this onto a wall? Your image on the wall must be the same size and the same way round as the cartoon; it would be uneconomic simply to copy it and the cartoon cannot be stuck on to the wall. CLUE – all the lines on the cartoon have lots of small holes pricked through them.

(The cartoon was held against the wall and chalk or charcoal was rubbed through all the holes to create a 'dot-to-dot' picture; the dots were then joined to re-create the image.)

This technique is called pouncing and was frequently used in Tudor portraiture to make copies (see Introduction). This is the only genuine drawing by Holbein of Henry VIII to have survived. There is only one authentic oil painting of Henry VIII by Holbein (now in Madrid); there are lots of other copies but none are definitely by Holbein (see **photocopy master 3**).

How long would you guess it took to complete the whole process, from starting the cartoon to finishing the wall painting?

(About a year.)

Focus on the missing part of the cartoon

Does the cartoon look as though it is complete? Look particularly at the position of Henry VII at the edge of it.

(No, part of it is missing beside Henry VII.)

Henry VII's wife, Elizabeth of York, was originally beside him; Henry VIII was depicted with the wife he was married to when the cartoon was started and who, unlike the rest of his wives, later gave birth to the child that Henry really wanted. Who was she?

(Jane Seymour, the mother of his son and heir.)

In the frieze at the top of the picture a mermaid and a merman hold a shield with lovers' knots and the initials 'H' and 'J'; whose names do you think they stand for?

(Henry and Jane.)

SI IUVAT HEROUM CLARAS VIDISSE FIGURAS,
SPECTA HAS, MAIORES NULLA TABELLA TULIT.
CERTAMEN MAGNUM LIS, QUESTIO MAGNA PATERNE,
FILIUS AN VINCAT. VICIT. UTERQUE QUIDEM.
ISTE SUOS HOSTES PATRIÆQUE INCENDIA SÆPE
SUSTULIT, ET PACEM CIVIBUS USQUE DEDIT.
FILIUS AD MAIORA QUIDEM PROGNATUS AB ARIS
SUBMOVET INDIGNOS, SUBSTITUITQUE PROBOS.
CERTÆ VIRTUTI, PAPARUM AUDACIA CESSIT,
HENRICO OCTAVO SCEPTRA GERENTE MANU
REDDITA RELIGIO EST, ISTO REGNANTE DEIQUE
DOGMATA CEPERUNT ESSE IN HONORE SUO.
FECIT HOLBENIUS IUBENTE HENRICO VIII.

This method worked well with smaller images. The huge drawing of Henry VIII and Henry VII is, however, evidence for another method of transfer. It has holes pricked through the paper along the outlines, just visible to the naked eye (see **photocopy master 4***). These suggest transfer by pouncing, allowing dust from a bag of charcoal dust, lightly banged over the surface, to penetrate the holes and transfer the pattern to the panel.*

By the time the wall painting was finished, three of the four people were already dead; how did Holbein include them?

(Jane Seymour from a portrait he had painted of her; Henry VII and Elizabeth of York from their tomb in Westminster Abbey – Elizabeth of York's tomb sculpture was itself made from a painting.)

Why do you think the part of the cartoon showing Henry VIII survived, while the rest was destroyed?

(It could be used again as a pattern to make other paintings of Henry; the other people were dead so there was less demand for their portraits.)

What is the picture all about?

(The Tudor family, dynasty, power of the monarchy.)

What sort of people would have seen the finished wall painting in Henry VIII's palace?

(Important visitors, nobles, ambassadors from abroad, etc.)

How would the majority of the King's subjects have seen what he looked like?

(From his image on the coinage.)

ACTIVITIES

1. Henry VIII has had a brilliant idea. He has seen just the right wall in Whitehall Palace on which to have painted a huge mural of himself and his family. He summons his painter Hans Holbein. Imagine the conversation between the King and his painter. It should include who will be represented in the picture, what sources Holbein should use for the images, practical details of how he will tackle such a large mural and a discussion about how Henry VIII should be portrayed in order to make him the dominant feature of the composition. This role-play clearly has comic as well as serious potential: at least one character must remain within the bounds of historical truth, though the other, if desired, could make present-day suggestions and be talked out of them by the historically-based character giving appropriate Tudor reasons.

2. Try out the two methods of copying described on page 8 and above:
   a) *Pouncing*: For this activity you will need photocopies of **master 4** to show pouncing holes and of **master 5** to complete the pouncing activity. Look at the dots made by pouncing around Henry's foot (**master 4**). Now take the

photocopy of Henry's head (**master 5**), place a sheet of tracing paper under it and prick through the lines with a darning needle or awl. (If preparing a class set, several sheets can be pricked at once.) Then place the tracing paper onto a clean sheet of paper and rub charcoal or dark chalk through the holes. The pictures can then be completed in colour.

b) *Tracing*: Cover a sheet of paper with dark chalk or charcoal and use it like carbon paper; place it under a drawing, with the chalk side facing down onto a blank piece of paper, and then trace over the lines.

A less messy method, though not as authentic, is to rub a layer of wax or oil crayon on top of the chalk layer. With the chalk/crayon layer facing upwards cover the sheet with a clean piece of paper. Place a drawing on top of both sheets and then trace over the lines. When finished remove the drawing and the clean sheet of paper from above the chalk/crayon layer. Where the lines have been traced the crayon will have been removed to reveal the chalk layer beneath, thereby creating a reverse-print effect.

3. Make a life-size version of the whole Whitehall mural using the photocopy master of the Leemput copy (**master 3**). Trace the outlines onto an OHP acetate sheet, project onto large sheets of paper on a wall, and draw around the outlines. Details and colour can also be added, either by further research into Tudor portraiture or by imaginative reconstructions. The National Portrait Gallery has a range of Tudor portraits on slide, poster and postcard – including packs with information – which would help with this project and which can be used to extend the painting to include the entire Tudor dynasty.

Sir Thomas More, his Father, Household and Descendants

By Rowland Lockey, partly after Hans Holbein, 1593

STRUCTURED DISCUSSION

Focus on how the picture was made

This portrait is very large – more than two metres high and three metres wide – what has it been painted on?

(Canvas, it would have been virtually impossible to have had a wooden panel this size.)

Do you think that a single piece of canvas this size could have been woven in Tudor times?

(No, it had to be joined. On the original a horizontal join can be seen between the painting of Anne Cresacre on the wall and the heads of the sitters.)

What kind of paint has been used?

(Oil paint.)

Focus on Thomas More

How has Thomas More (second man from left) been made to stand out?

(By his gold chain.)

What shows that he served King Henry VIII?

(Tudor rose on the chain.)

How does the fabric of Thomas More's clothes differ from that of the robes worn by his father, sitting on his right?

(Thomas More wears velvet, seen most clearly on his sleeves; his father was a judge and judicial robes were woollen.)

Focus on the history of the painting

The people around Thomas More are wearing clothes from the time of Henry VIII; with which monarch do you associate the clothes of the four people to the right of the picture?

(Elizabeth I.)

What is distinctively Elizabethan about these clothes?

(The ruffs.)

In whose reign, therefore, would you say that this picture was painted?

(Elizabeth I's.)

What was the artist's source for the figures from Henry VIII's reign?

(An earlier picture, which he copied.)

INTRODUCTION

*The More family group portrait was the most ambitious work painted by Holbein during his first visit to England in 1526 to 1528. The original was destroyed in the 18th century, but various copies have survived. One of these is the National Portrait Gallery's version by Rowland Lockey (***poster 3***), which includes Elizabethan descendants of Thomas More. More's unshakeable adherence to Roman Catholicism clashed with Henry VIII's more secular ambitions. He refused to take the oath under the Act of Supremacy and was executed in 1535, declaring that he was 'the King's good servant, but God's first'.*

After Sir Thomas More's execution his goods were dispersed, but in 1590 his grandson, also called Thomas, was able to buy back Holbein's family group painting. He then commissioned three copies of it. One was a straightforward copy, now at Nostell Priory, Yorkshire. Two used the original for the deceased family members, but excluded non-blood relations, and added those living in 1593. **Poster 3** *shows one of these (the other, a miniature version, is in the Victoria and Albert Museum, London). It commemorates the continuing belief of the family* ➳

in the Catholic faith, associating the martyred Sir Thomas with the Mores living in 1593, who are easily identifiable by their ruffs.

It is possible to tell, simply by looking at the figures that date from the reign of Henry VIII, that their positions have been moved around and that this is not just a direct copy of Holbein's group.

Look at Elizabeth Dauncy, who is the lady in early Tudor dress standing sixth from the left and looking to the right of the picture. She would appear very odd if she were placed close to the edge of the picture, staring out of it. Where would be a more sensible place to put her, in this pose, among her family?

(The obvious place for her would be on the far left beside Sir John More – who wears bright red – where she would give a clear defining edge to the group and would look across, rather than away from, her family. This is, in fact, where she was in Holbein's painting.)

Focus on the More family

Why did the Elizabethan Mores want their ancestor Thomas More in the picture?

(Because he was a famous scholar and a Roman Catholic martyr and to show their descent from him.)

The girl on the left of Thomas More, Anne Cresacre, appears again in the painting; where is she portrayed?

(In the portrait hanging on the wall behind.)

By looking at her in the portrait on the wall, can you tell what has happened to her husband?

(She is dressed as a widow, so he has died.)

Anne Cresacre was fifteen or sixteen when she was painted in the original picture; why do you think she was portrayed twice?

(To show her as a woman, as well as a girl: she is a key figure in the family's descent, continuing to bring up her children in the Roman Catholic faith.)

From the evidence of this picture, what interests do the More family have?

(Music, reading, flowers, portraits, heraldry.)

What evidence is there that they were interested in technology?

(The clock, which we might take for granted but it was technologically advanced for its day.)

What were the main characteristics of life in the More household, as shown in this picture?

(Wealth, comfort, closeness, education and importance of women, peace and calm, religion, literature, music, etc.)

ACTIVITIES

1. Create your own family group using photographs; how many generations can you include? Try using the compositional framework of *Thomas More, his Father, Household and Descendants* by tracing loosely around the outline of the poster and then filling it in with likenesses of your own relatives. Who would be appropriate to put where? Can you use the framework to show relationships between family members?

2. Focus on the meaning-bearing objects and the symbols in *Thomas More, his Father, Household and Descendants* (for example, books, flowers, crucifix, etc.). Then design a self-portrait which uses objects and symbols appropriate to yourself (for example, football colours, badges for membership of clubs and societies, items connected with hobbies or interests, etc.). How many messages about yourself can you convey?

3. *Thomas More, his Father, Household and Descendants* depicts a wide range of Tudor fabrics, from the velvet on Thomas More's sleeve and the wool of his father's gown to the fine gauze of the ruffs. Use the picture as the starting point for work on representing the textures of different fabrics, comparing it with samples of real fabric and your own depictions of fabric textures.

Elizabeth I

By Marcus Gheeraerts the Younger, c.1592

INTRODUCTION

The French Ambassador, writing a few years after this portrait was painted, said of Elizabeth 'As for her face, it is and appears to be very aged. It is long and thin, and her teeth are very yellow and many of them are missing. Her figure is fair and tall and graceful whatever she does.' Marcus Gheeraerts has balanced flattery with realism to produce this image of the ageing queen.

The picture is filled with symbolism. Elizabeth's white dress reflects her virginity, while the rose pinned to her ruff represents beauty and the House of Tudor. The map of England beneath her feet displays her domination over her kingdom; standing on the globe suggests her aspiration to Imperial power. The strange mixture of weather – storms and sunshine – recalls that she has successfully brought her country through troubled times to its present happy state. As well as these political symbols, the picture has a personal message too: the portrait commemorates Elizabeth's forgiveness of one of her courtiers, Sir Henry Lee, for having taken a mistress. It is on Lee's house in Oxfordshire that she is standing on the map and which gives the portrait its usual title of the 'Ditchley Portrait' of Elizabeth I. The painting seems to have ➳

STRUCTURED DISCUSSION

Focus on her face

How old do you think Elizabeth is?

(She is fifty-nine, people generally guess that she is younger than this.)

How has the painter made her seem younger?

(Hair colour, lack of wrinkles.)

Are there any signs of ageing?

(Bags under her eyes, a few lines on her face.)

Why might she have wanted to look younger than she really was?

(Personal vanity; also political reasons: she controls her court through the fiction that her courtiers are all in love with her and it was dangerous to appear old and weak as this might have encouraged challenges from younger claimants to the throne.)

Why is her hair this colour?

(It is a wig.)

What is odd about her mouth and why?

(It is very small, she has lost most of her teeth.)

Focus on the background

What is under her feet?

(A map of England.)

Why?

(She rules it.)

What is the map on?

(A globe.)

Why?

(Claiming Imperial power; it refers to her stature as a ruler.)

What can you see in the sea?

(Ships and sea monsters.)

Why might they be there?

(Possible reference to the Armada, to exploration; also a conventional map decoration of the time.)

Describe the weather in the picture.

(Storms to the right, sunshine to the left.)

been made for Elizabeth's first visit to Lee's house after her two year absence while he was out of favour. The storms and sunshine refer to the quarrel and reconciliation, Elizabeth putting her anger, represented by the storm, behind her.

Elizabeth is standing on Ditchley, the house of her courtier, Sir Henry Lee. This picture, known as the 'Ditchley Portrait', was painted for Henry Lee, the Queen's champion from 1559 to 1590, and commemorates Elizabeth's visit to Lee's house at Ditchley near Oxford in September 1592. Lee had incurred Elizabeth's anger by taking a mistress, Anne Vavasour. The Queen's visit to Ditchley in 1592 was a sign that she had forgiven him for his love of Anne.

Which way is Elizabeth facing?

(Towards the sunny side.)

What might the weather be saying about Elizabeth's reign?

(She has brought her country through difficult times – such as the Armada – to its present happy state.)

Focus on her body and clothes

Is there any other obvious sign of flattery in this portrait?

(The waist is unnaturally thin.)

What is the significance of the colour of her dress?

(Idea of virginity/purity, like a wedding dress.)

Who or what might she be married to?

(The country under her feet.)

What has been used to decorate her dress?

(Pearls, gold, jewels; a dress like this would be extremely costly, around £500,000 at today's prices.)

What has she got pinned to her ruff and why?

(A pink rose which is a symbol of beauty and of the House of Tudor.)

What is Elizabeth holding in her hands?

(Fan in her right hand; gloves in her left.)

Can you link these to the weather in this picture?

(Fan for sunny weather; gloves for stormy weather.)

Would it be comfortable to wear a dress like this?

(No, it would be very heavy.)

Do you think she was always dressed like this?

(No, she is wearing her 'best' clothes for a portrait, as we might today for a photograph; she often actually wore a looser robe like a dressing gown.)

If you met her wearing this dress, would you be able to see her feet?

(No.)

Why has the painter shown her feet in this portrait? CLUE – look at what she is standing on.

(To show her at a particular place on the map.)

Can you link the weather in this portrait to the Queen's quarrel and forgiveness of Lee?

(Storms for the quarrel; sunshine for forgiveness.)

Focus on the painting itself

What is this portrait painted on, and with what?

(On canvas, with oil paint.)

Are you seeing the whole portrait as it was originally painted?

(No, the edges have been cut down; this is especially clear along the right edge where part of the writing is missing.)

Why might this have been done?

(To fit the portrait into a smaller space.)

ACTIVITIES

1. Use face paints to create the Elizabethan idea of beauty. Make the face as white as possible, redden the lips and cheeks and then draw blue veins on the temples, starting at the end of the eyebrows. The eyebrows should be concealed as far as possible (a real Elizabethan lady would have plucked hers). Take the hair back off the face to expose as much forehead as possible (again, this might have been plucked). Do the children think a face with Elizabethan make-up looks beautiful?

2. On a clay tile – 20 to 30 cm square – create an image of Elizabeth I in relief. Mould the features of her face (clay pushed through a fine sieve makes excellent hair). Make patterns to decorate her clothes and add details of the background. If you are adding decoration with separate pieces of clay, stick them on firmly with very wet clay (called slip). Dry the finished relief slowly, fire in a kiln and then glaze and fire again.

3. Elizabeth I was extremely concerned about how she looked, particularly as she aged. She insisted that artists used her approved face pattern drawing. Get half the class to pounce pictures of Elizabeth (see pages 8 and 10 for further instructions) using the pattern provided (**photocopy master 6**) and the other half to copy Elizabeth direct from the poster. Which method produces more accurate pictures of Elizabeth? Which method shows more of the artist's individuality? Which would Elizabeth have wanted? Which do we like better?

Sir Francis Drake

By an unknown artist, c.1580–1585

INTRODUCTION

This portrait represents Sir Francis Drake after his famous circumnavigation of the world, for which he was knighted in 1581, but before the Spanish Armada. The details – the globe, and his coat of arms with God's hand leading the ship – therefore relate particularly to his historic voyage.

The portrait itself has had a varied past. At some point it has been extended both at the top and the bottom. At another time it was cut down to create a head and shoulders portrait, but it has now been reinstated into a full-length portrait. There are few paintings of Drake, partly because his poor origins meant that there were no early portraits made and also, perhaps, because he spent considerable time away at sea.

STRUCTURED DISCUSSION

Focus on the globe

What is Drake famous for?

(Voyage around the world, fighting the Armada. He became rich from plundering foreign ships.)

This picture was painted before the Armada, but after his voyage around the world; how is his famous voyage shown in the portrait?

(By his hand on the globe.)

Can you see any parts of the world on the globe?

(The continent of Africa is under his thumb, with Europe below it and India in the centre. The globe is upside down; globes were still uncommon in Elizabethan times so it is possible that the artist got muddled and painted the globe upside down by mistake.)

Focus on Drake

How does he show that he is rich?

(He is wearing a fine suit with fashionable slashing on the doublet and sleeves of his shirt, and a ruff. There is a coat of arms. He had a large portrait painted.)

How does he show he is a fighting man?

(He has a long sword on his left and a dagger on the other side.)

Would he have dressed like this when he was travelling and exploring?

(Unlikely, except for the sword.)

Why is he wearing two pairs of shoes?

(The dark pair are protective slippers over his smart indoor shoes.)

Focus on the coat of arms

(For larger groups, it may be more practical to use a photocopy of **master 7** for this part of the discussion.)

What represents the sea on his coat of arms?

(The waves across the middle.)

He has also chosen stars; why are they important to a sailor?

(For navigation.)

Look at the crest above the coat of arms. What can you see?

(There is a hand coming out of a cloud, holding strings attached to a ship on top of a globe.)

Whose hand is it?

(God's.)

Whose ship is it?

(Drake's.)

What does the crest mean?

(Drake's ship and his voyage had divine guidance.)

If you were a Spaniard would you have thought that Drake's ship was led by God?

(No.)

What language is below the coat of arms?

(Latin.)

‘*Sic parvis magna*’ means ‘greatness out of small things’ and relates to the story of Drake's life. His origins were quite humble and he became rich and powerful. He was given the coat of arms when he was knighted.

Why do you think it is in Latin?

(Latin was the language of educated Europeans. We still use it for mottoes. Has your school got one?)

ACTIVITIES

1. Look at the floor in the portrait. Using colour pencils, draw the pattern of this floor on to squared paper. Use one of your squares to be one black square on the floor. Make the brown square three squares long on each side.

   How many squares are in the brown square? (*9. This is called the area.*) How many white squares do you need to go round one brown square? (*12. This is called the perimeter.*) Which needs more squares, the brown area or the white perimeter? Using the same floor pattern draw the tiles again, but this time make the brown square four squares long on each side. The size of the black square should remain as one square. Increase the size of the white perimeter to fit around the brown square. Count up the brown area and the white perimeter; what has happened? (*Area is 16. Perimeter is 16.*) Now make the brown square five squares long on each side

SIC PARVIS MAGNA

(keeping the size of the black square as one square). What has happened to the area of the brown square and the perimeter? (*Area is 25. Perimeter is 20.*) What would happen if you further increased the size of the brown square? Can you find any pattern in the numbers you have generated? (*Area of the brown square: 9, 16, 25...; size of the perimeter: 12, 16, 20...*) Work out what the area of the brown square and the size of the perimeter would be if you continued to add squares to the brown square.

2. Look at the photocopy of Drake's coat of arms (**master 7**). Now make your own. Choose objects that will tell people about you and your interests, like Drake did. Choose a crest to go at the top and invent a motto (in English) which sums up what you think about your life.

Sir Henry Unton

By an unknown artist, c.1596

INTRODUCTION

The Unton memorial portrait is the only surviving example of a painting telling the entire story of a Tudor person's life. While it is not a great work of art – it was probably made by someone who did heraldic painting – it contains a wealth of interesting historical detail.

It was probably commissioned by Dorothy Unton after her husband's death in 1596. It follows several pictorial conventions which reflect medieval rather than Renaissance traditions. It is far from naturalistic and does not attempt to depict real space: the geography of Europe is telescoped so that Italy, the Low Countries and France are shown side by side, while the Alps are represented by four peaks; each time Henry Unton appears in a scene he is depicted far larger than the people around him; despite the passage of several decades in the events shown, everyone appears in the costume of the late 1590s.

The picture also has a strong symbolic content. The English Channel, as well as separating England from mainland Europe, serves as the river of life which runs from East to West across the painting, flowing out into the Sea of Eternity. The whole ⋙→

STRUCTURED DISCUSSION

Focus on his early life

Where is the section in which Henry Unton is a baby?

(Bottom-right-hand corner as you look at the painting.)

Who is holding him?

(His mother.)

He was educated at Oxford; where can you find him in this section of the picture?

(Indoors, with his hat on.)

> Henry Unton's mother was a more important person than his father (who does not appear in the painting); notice the coat of arms and the coronet above her head.

Focus on his travels

He then travelled abroad; what is the country he visited where there are cities called Venice and Padua?

(Italy.)

What was the weather like?

(Hot and sunny.)

What was Henry Unton carrying?

(A parasol.)

He then travelled to the Low Countries; what did he do there?

(Fought as a soldier.)

Where did he sleep on this expedition?

(In tents.)

> Unton was fighting against the Spanish and was knighted for his bravery at the Battle of Zutphen by the Earl of Leicester.

Focus on his house

What is happening in the middle of his house?

(People are having a meal.)

Can you see any cutlery?

(No, they used fingers at this time.)

What entertainment are they watching? (See colour detail on back cover.)

(Dancing.)

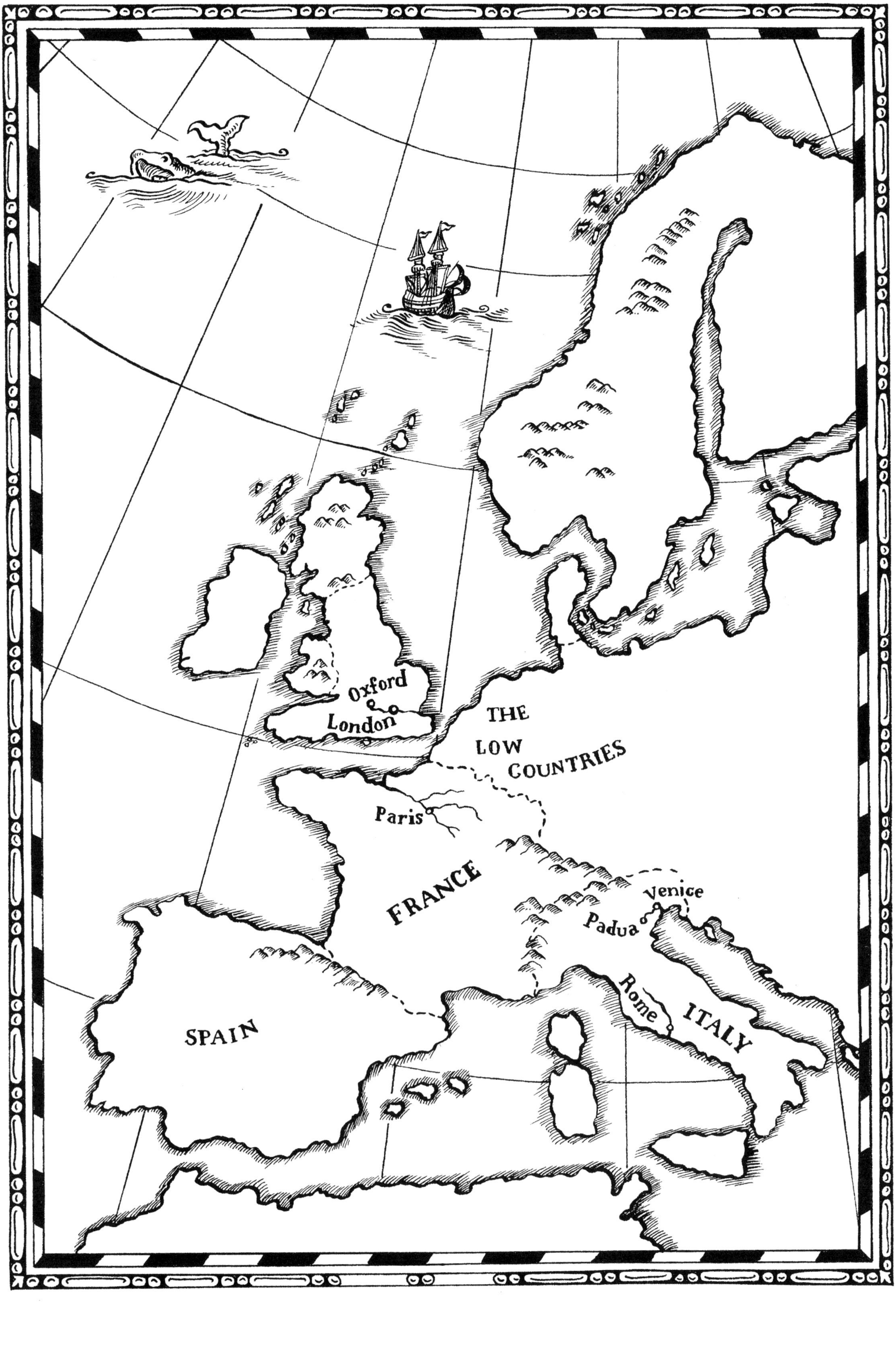

Oxford
London
THE
LOW
COUNTRIES
Paris
FRANCE
Venice
Padua
SPAIN
Rome
ITALY

picture is divided into two unequal parts, with life to the East and death, the larger section, to the West. Despite this asymmetrical division there are symbols which balance each other: the sun and the moon in the corners, the skeleton and the winged figure of Fame, and the doves of peace balancing the ravens of death to the right of the large portrait of Unton. Particularly striking is the amount of space devoted to Unton's death and burial, a reminder that death was far more uncertain and more central to every day life in Tudor England. Unton himself was barely forty years old when he died.

What musical instruments can you see?

(Lute, viols (like violins and cellos), flute, mandolin, drum.)

What are the women dancers wearing on their faces and heads?

(Red masks with long blonde wigs.)

What musical instrument is Henry Unton playing in one of the rooms to the left of the dining hall?

(The bass viol.)

> It is not known for sure whether or not the black children are really white children in black costumes and make-up.

The four men in black, to the left of the dining hall, are discussing religion; what is the big book one of them is holding?

(The Bible.)

In which part of the house is Henry Unton's study?

(The attic.)

Focus again on his travels

How did Henry Unton travel in France?

(On horseback.)

> Henry Unton went as ambassador from Elizabeth I to the French King.

What happened to him in France? (See colour detail on inside back cover.)

(He became ill.)

What is the red stuff in the bowls by his bedside?

(Blood.)

> The Tudors believed that taking blood reduced the temperature. The French King sent his own doctor to treat Henry Unton.

What is the doctor doing?

(Taking Unton's pulse.)

Did Henry Unton get better?

(No, he died.)

What is the skeleton carrying?

(An hourglass.)

How was Unton's body brought back for his funeral?

(On a ship with black sails, then by cart.)

What did people wear to Unton's funeral?

(Long black cloaks with hoods.)

What sort of people are climbing on the wall at the front?

(Poorer people who have come to see the funeral.)

Where is there any colour apart from black in the funeral procession?

(In the heraldry: on the coffin, on the herald's tabards and on the banners.)

Henry Unton was given a specially grand funeral because he died whilst Elizabeth I's ambassador.

Unton's tomb was really inside the church; why has the artist put it outside?

(So you can see it.)

Who is the woman behind Henry Unton on his tomb?

(Dorothy, his wife.)

Focus on the large portrait of Henry Unton

How can you tell from his clothes that he lived in Elizabethan times?

(He wears a ruff.)

He is also wearing Queen Elizabeth's portrait; where is it?

(On a chain round his neck.)

ACTIVITIES

1. Make pictures showing all the different stages of your own life, starting with your birth and picking out events of particular importance. Imagine what will happen to you when you get older.

2. Imagine you are Henry Unton on one of his journeys abroad. Write a letter or journal entry from one of his travels abroad.

3. Plot Henry Unton's journey on the Tudor map of Europe (**photocopy master 8**). Did he have to go through any countries that are not shown in the picture? Do the countries on the map look the same as the countries in the picture? Does the Tudor map look the same as a modern map of Europe?